WORLD'S BEST
CARD GAMES
FOR ONE

WORLD'S BEST CARD GAMES

FOR ONE

SHEILA ANNE BARRY
ILLUSTRATED BY MYRON MILLER

Sterling Publishing Co., Inc.   New York

Other Books in the Same Series

101 Best Family Card Games
World's Best Card Tricks
World's Best Magic Tricks
World's Best Outdoor Games
World's Best Party Games
World's Best Street & Yard Games
World's Best String Games
World's Best Travel Games

Library of Congress Cataloging-in-Publication Data

Barry, Sheila Anne.
    World's best card games for one / by Sheila Anne Barry ;
illustrated by Myron Miller.
        p.   cm.
    Includes index.
    ISBN 0-8069-8636-0
    1. Solitaire (Game)   I. Title.
GV1261.B33   1992
795.4'3—dc20   92-21866
                                                      CIP

10 9 8 7 6 5 4 3 2

First paperback edition published in 1993 by
Sterling Publishing Company, Inc.
387 Park Avenue South, New York, N.Y. 10016
© 1992 by Sheila Anne Barry
Distributed in Canada by Sterling Publishing
% Canadian Manda Group, P.O. Box 920, Station U
Toronto, Ontario, Canada M8Z 5P9
Distributed in Great Britain and Europe by Cassell PLC
Villiers House, 41/47 Strand, London WC2N 5JE, England
Distributed in Australia by Capricorn Link Ltd.
P.O. Box 665, Lane Cove, NSW 2066
Manufactured in the United States of America
All rights reserved

Sterling ISBN 0-8069-8636-0 Trade
                0-8069-8637-9 Paper

Contents

Two-Pack Games

A Word About Great Games _____

What makes the games in this book the world's best?

First, every one of them has something about it that is intriguing and challenging—something that makes it especially enjoyable to play. Tedious, cumbersome, colorless games have been weeded out.

- You'll find simple counting games that are just right for when you don't want to be overtaxed.
- You'll find complex games that call on every bit of your concentration.
- You'll find games that are irresistible because they have such a great look to them.
- And many are so mesmerizing and compelling that once you start playing them, you can't stop.

Second, all the games are practical. You won't find layouts that you'd have to play on the floor or that require your handling three or four decks of cards.

Third, the ratio between the number of cards you need to lay out and the amount of play in the game is usually a comfortable one. You don't have to lay out two packs of cards only to discover that the game is lost before you even get to make a move! Most of those infuriating games have been eliminated, unless they have a particular fascination of their own—and then you're warned in advance.

All the games that did get into the book are worth trying out—and fun to play. We hope you like them as much as we do, and find a few that become your new favorites.

Before You Begin _____

We've grouped the one-pack and two-pack games separately, on the supposition that you probably have only one pack at hand most of the time.

The descriptions at the top of each game will let you know vital information right away—which games are possible to play in a very small area, for example.

They will also tell you which games are easy to win and which are almost impossible—so you know what you're up against.

We've tried to eliminate words that you have to go back and look up, like "reserve" and "tableaux," so you can whip through the instructions and start to play right away.

But there are a few terms you need to be familiar with:

- *Suit*—There are four of them: Hearts, Diamonds, Clubs, and Spades.
- *Suite*—A full set of thirteen cards of one suit: Ace to King of Clubs, for example.
- *To build*—To place one card on another to create a sequence—whatever kind is called for. Usually the sequence just goes up or down—the Queen, for example, is placed on the King if the sequence is down, on the Jack if it's up.
- *Building upward in suit* means laying down cards from low to high—from the Ace (or wherever you have to start from)—to the King (or wherever you have to end at)—in one single suit: from the Ace to the King of Hearts, for instance.
- *Building downward in suit* means laying down cards from high to low—from the King of Hearts through the ranks to the Ace, for example.
- *Rank*—The card's number. A 10 of Diamonds "ranks" higher than a 9 of Diamonds.

- *Foundations*—The cards that score—the ones you build on. They are usually put up above the layout, as in the most popular solitaire games, *Klondike* and *Canfield*. But sometimes they are placed differently—or not placed at all.
- *The stockpile*—The cards that are left in your hand after you have completed the layout.
- *The wastepile*—The collection of discarded cards.
- *A column*—Cards that go vertically in a line.
- *A row*—Cards that go horizontally in a line.
- *Deuces*—2s.

Games are arranged alphabetically, but when talking about a prototype game, we've placed the best variations next to it, so that you don't have to leaf back to find the rules for the original game.

Every layout is shown in the book, except when the variations follow a prototype game—or when there's no layout at all, as in *Hit or Miss*.

Solitaire is really the ultimate game—one in which it is very clear that you are competing only against yourself and the run of the cards (sort of like Life?). Win or not, we hope you enjoy playing the games!

One-Pack Games

Accordion

Other Names: Idle Year
Tower of Babel
Methuselah
Space: Small/Moderate
Level: Difficult

Play: Start by dealing the cards one at a time face up in a row of four from left to right. Go slowly so that you can keep comparing the cards you deal with their neighbors. Whenever a card matches the card on its left—or third to the left—you move the new card over onto the one it matches. The match may be in suit or rank.

Let's say that the first four cards you turn up are:

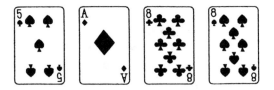

The 8 of Spades matches the 8 of Clubs (on its left) and also the 5 of Spades (third to the left). You could move it onto either one. Which one will turn out better? You really can't tell at this point.

Once you move a card over, though, the card on the bottom doesn't have any more significance. The card on top is the one to match.

As soon as you move a card—or a pile—move the later cards over to close up the sequence. That will open up new moves for you, too.

Go on dealing cards, one at a time, stopping after each one to make whatever moves are possible, until you've used up all the cards.

For example, suppose that you deal:

   You can move the 2 of Clubs onto the 2 of Hearts. Then close up the row. The 5 of Clubs moves next to the 2s. It's a Club and that's a match! But once you move the 5 over onto the 2 of Clubs, another move opens up: You can move the entire pile over onto the 5 of Spades, which is the third card to the left. So the cards look like this:

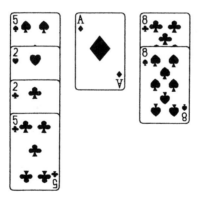

To win the game: Get the whole pack into one pile. It's almost impossible. If you end up with five piles, you're doing pretty well.

Aces Up

Other Names: Idiot's Delight
Firing Squad

Space: Small
Level: Moderate

Layout: Deal four cards in a row.

Play: If you have two cards of the same suit, discard the one that is lower in rank. Aces are high. For example, here you have:

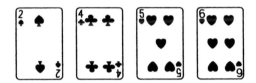

Discard the 5 of Hearts.

When you've made all the moves you can, fill the empty space in the row with any top card from the layout. In this case, where there is only one layer of cards as yet, fill the space from the cards in your hand. Then deal four more cards overlapping the ones you've already set up.

Go through the same process of discarding the lower card of the same suit from the new layer of cards.

And so on until you've gone through the whole pack.

To win the game: Discard all the cards—except the Aces, of course.

Auld Lang Syne

Other Names: **Patience**
Space: **Small**
Level: **Very Difficult**

Layout: Deal out all four Aces in a row. Underneath each one, deal a card. These cards are the stock from which you are going to build.

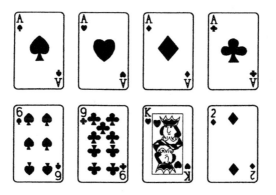

To win the game: Build the Aces up to Kings, regardless of suit.

Play: When you've finished the moves you can make with the first set of four cards, deal another row of four right on top of them. Keep going until the stock is exhausted.

Tam O'Shanter

Level: **Almost Impossible**

Play in exactly the same way as *Auld Lang Syne*, except don't put the Aces up first. Just wait until they show up in the deal.

Baker's Dozen

Other Names: None
Space: Wide
Level: Easy

Layout: Deal 13 columns of four overlapping cards. Aces will go into a foundation row above the layout.

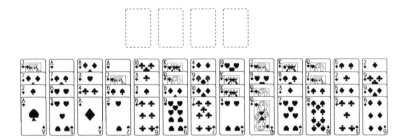

After you lay out the cards, check on the Kings. If a King is in an exposed position, move it underneath the other cards in the column. If a King is lying on another card of the same suit, place it underneath that card.

To win the game: Release Aces and build them up to Kings in suit.

Play: Build downward on the cards in the layout, one card at a time, regardless of color or suit. Do not fill any spaces.

Perseverance

Level: Moderate

Play exactly the same way as *Baker's Dozen*, except:
1. Set Aces in foundation piles from the start.
2. Lay out twelve columns of four overlapping cards each.
3. If a group of cards is in suit and in sequence, starting at the top, you can move the entire sequence as a unit.

4. On the layout, build down in suit only.
5. You have two **redeals**. Gather up the piles in the reverse order of the way you put them down, and then deal them back into twelve columns, as far as they go.

Good Measure

Play exactly the same way as *Baker's Dozen*, except:
1. Deal ten columns of five overlapping cards.
2. Start with two Aces in the foundation row.

Baroness

Other Names: **Thirteen**
Five Piles
Space: **Moderate**
Level: **Easy/Moderate**

Layout: Deal a row of five cards.

Play: Remove any Kings or any pair of cards that add up to 13. That includes not only:

3 and 10	5 and 8
4 and 9	6 and 7

but also: Ace and Queen and 2 and Jack.

Discard those cards. Then deal the next row of five, on top of the first one, and go through the same process. Only the top cards are available for pairing and discarding.

Deal on, until the pack has been exhausted. The two cards left over at the end can be made into a separate pile. They are also available to be paired and discarded.

To win the game: Discard all the cards in pairs that add up to 13.

Redeals: None.

Beleaguered Castle

Other Names: Laying Siege
Sham Battle

Space Large
Level: Easy

Layout: Lay out the cards in two large wings, each made up of four rows of six overlapping cards.

In the middle, place a column of Aces—the foundations.

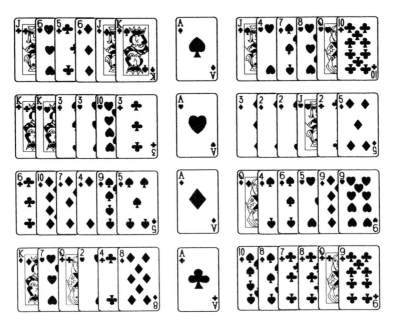

There is a traditional way to lay out the cards:

    Start with the Aces in a column in the middle. Then deal out a column of four cards along the left-hand side and a column of four cards at the right-hand side. Then alternate in dealing columns, left and right, until the pack is all laid down.

To win the game: Build the Aces up to Kings in suit.

Play: The only cards that may be moved onto the foundations are the completely exposed ones on the ends of the wings. The cards on the ends can also be moved onto each other, regardless of suit, going downward in rank. For instance, in the example above, the 9 of Hearts could go on the 10 of Spades, but not on the 8 of Diamonds.

    Should any row in the wing become empty, you can fill it with any exposed card.

Streets and Alleys _____

Play exactly the same way as *Beleaguered Castle*, except:
1. Do not set up the Aces ahead of time, but mix them in with the pack.
2. Deal seven cards to the two top rows of the wings on each side.

Citadel _____

Play in exactly the same way as *Beleaguered Castle*, except:
1. Do not set up the Aces ahead of time, but mix them in with the pack.
2. During the process of dealing, you may play any cards to the foundations that they are ready to receive. Once an

Ace is in place, for example, you may fill in with deuces, and if deuces are there, you could even build 3s or higher.

When a card is placed on a foundation during the dealing, do not replace it in the layout; just leave its space empty.

3. When dealing, once a card is laid down on the wings, it cannot be moved until the dealing is over.

Betrothal

Other Names: **Royal Marriage**
Coquette
Matrimony

Space: **Large**
Level: **Easy**

To win the game: Get the Queen of Hearts next to the King of Hearts. And while you try to do this, you eliminate some of the spoilsports who come between other "like" couples.

Layout: Start with the Queen of Hearts at your left. Put the King of Hearts at the bottom of the deck. Deal the cards in a row, one by one, next to the Queen, until the whole pack is out on the table.

Play: While you deal, however, you can throw out certain cards—any one or two cards that get between two cards of the same rank or suit.

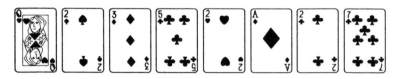

For example, in the layout on page 22, which you've just started, you can remove the 3 of Diamonds and the 5 of Clubs, because they are between two cards of the same rank, the 2s. You can also remove the Ace of Diamonds because it lies between two cards of the same suit (2s again).

Betsy Ross

Other Names: **Musical**   **Plus Belle**
                      Fairest   **Four Kings**
                      Quadruple Alliance
Space: **Small**
Level: **Moderate**

Lay out on the table any Ace, 2, 3, and 4. Directly under them lay out any 2, 4, 6, and 8. The four cards on the bottom are foundations. You'll be building on them, but in an odd sort of way.

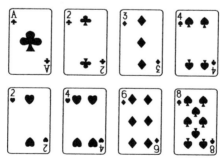

The only purpose of the top row is to remind you of the key numbers you have to build by.

On the 2 you'll build the standard way—by 1s:
2 3 4 5 6 7 8 9 10 J Q K

On the 4 you'll build by 2s:
4 6 8 10 Q A 3 5 7 9 J K

On the 6 you'll build by 3s:
6 9 Q 2 5 8 J A 4 7 10 K

On the 8 you'll build by 4s:
8 Q 3 7 J 2 6 10 A 5 9 K

To win the game: Build all the cards into groups of 13 on the foundations.
Redeals: Two.

Bisley

Other Names: None
Space: Very wide
Level: Moderate

Layout: Remove the Aces from the pack and deal them onto the table as the first four cards in a row of 13. The next nine cards in the pack are then dealt next to them but lower down.

Go on to create three more rows of 13 until all the cards are laid out.

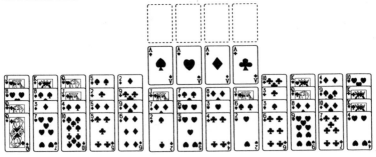

To win the game: Build Aces up to Kings in suit and Kings down to Aces.

Play: As they become available, remove the Kings and place them above the Aces. Build on the cards in the layout, upward or downward in suit, playing any cards that you can to the foundations.

Calculation

Other Names: **Broken Intervals**
                The Fairest
Space: **Small**
Level: **Easy**

Layout: Remove any Ace, 2, 3, and 4 from the pack and set them up in a row. They are your foundations.

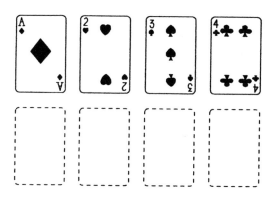

To win the game: Build up all the foundations to Kings, each in a different way.

Play: The first card, the Ace, will be built by 1s—the same way you've been building Aces straight along—
1 2 3 4 5 6 7 8 9 10 J Q K

The second card—the 2—will be built by 2s—

2 4 6 8 10 Q A 3 5 7 9 J K

The third card—the 3—will be built by 3s—

3 6 9 Q 2 5 8 J A 4 7 10 K

The fourth card—the 4—will be built by 4s—

4 8 Q 3 7 J 2 6 10 A 5 9 K

Start by turning over one card at a time, which you can build, regardless of suit, on any foundation that is ready for it. If the card cannot be used on any pile, put it in one of four possible wastepiles underneath the foundations. The top cards of the wastepiles are available to play onto the foundations. The strategy you use to decide where to place an unusable card is crucial. It's okay to keep the cards spread out so you can see what your choices are at any moment.

Canfield

Other Names: Fascination
                 Thirteen
                 Demon
Space: Small
Level: Difficult

Canfield is one of the most popular solitaire games in the world. A shorter, faster game than *Klondike*, Canfield is played much the same way, but it starts from a different basic layout.

Canfield came by its name in an interesting way. Mr. Canfield owned a gambling house in Saratoga Springs in the 1890s. He used to sell his customers packs of cards at $50 each and then pay them back $5 for every card they were able to score. Estimates are that the average number of cards you could expect to score in a game was five or six, so Mr. Canfield did pretty well.

Layout: Count out 13 cards into one pile and put it in front of you face up and a little to your left. Then put a 14th card to the right of the pile and slightly above it; whatever that card is, it becomes the foundation card of this particular deal. As the other cards of the same rank appear, you'll be placing them too in the foundation row.

To win the game: Build the foundation cards into four complete suits of 13 cards each.

Next, you lay out a row of four cards below the foundation card, face up:

No cards are ever built on the 13-pile. The object is to unload it. For example, in the illustration above, you couldn't put a 5—or any other card—on the 6. Cards from the 13-pile can be played only onto the foundations or into the four-card row when a space opens up.

Play: First check the four-card spread carefully to see whether you can make any moves. Besides playing cards to the foundations, you can build cards onto the four-card spread downward in alternating colors.

For instance, in the illustration above, the 3 of Hearts can go onto the 4 of Spades; the 7 of Diamonds can go up into the foundation row; and the 6 of Spades can come down into the row of four. Once it does, the 5 of Hearts can be played onto it.

You are permitted to move sequences of cards as one unit. For example, the 3 and 4 may be moved together onto the 5 and 6, so your layout would look like this:

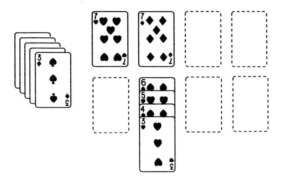

Then you can proceed to fill the other open spaces in the four-card row with cards from the 13-pile.

Now start turning up cards from the pack, in batches of three, playing them either to the foundations, to the four-card row, or to the wastepile. The top card of the wastepile is always available for play.

As spaces open up in the four-card row, continue to fill them with cards from the 13-card pile. When these are exhausted, you can fill them with cards from your hand or from the wastepile.

Redeal: As many times as you want, or until the game is blocked.

Selective Canfield _____

Play exactly the same way as *Canfield*, except deal a five-card row instead of four. Choose your foundation yourself from one of these cards.

Rainbow

Play exactly the same way as *Canfield*, except go through the pack one card at a time. You are allowed two **redeals** in some versions of the game—none in others!

Storehouse

Other Names: **Provisions**
                        Thirteen Up
                        Reserve
Space: **Small**
Level: **Easy**

Play exactly the same way as *Canfield*, except:
1. Remove the four deuces from the pack and set them up as the foundations.
2. Build them up in suit to Aces.

Superior Demon

Level: **Moderate**

Play exactly the same way as *Canfield*, except:
1. Spread the 13-card pile so that you can see it and take it into account as you play.
2. You don't have to fill a space in the layout until you want.
3. You can shift any part of a sequence to another position—you don't have to move the entire sequence.

Chameleon

Play in exactly the same way as *Canfield*, except:
1. Count out only 12 cards instead of 13 for the 13-card pile.
2. Deal only three cards to the four-card row.
3. The layout looks slightly different, like this:

The Clock

Other Names:	Hidden Cards	Sundial
	Four of a Kind	All Fours
	Travellers	Hunt

Space: Moderate
Level: Difficult

Deal the pack into 13 face-down piles of four cards each.

Arrange 12 of them in a circle, representing the numbers on a clock dial. Put the 13th pile in the middle of the circle. It should look like this:

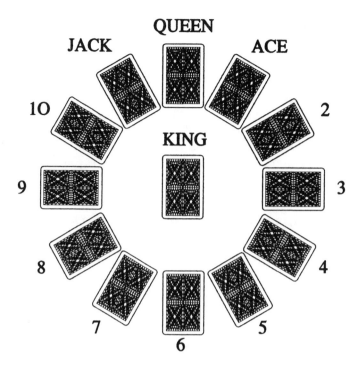

Start by picking up the top card of the middle pile. Suppose it's a 5. Slip it, face up, under the pile of cards that are in the 5 o'clock position. Then pick up the top card of the 5 o'clock pile. Suppose it's a Jack. It would go under the 11 o'clock pile (remember, the King pile is in the middle of the clock—and the Queen is at 12). And you would pick up the top card of the 11 o'clock pile and slip it under whatever pile it belongs in.

When you slip the fourth card of any group into place— and there is no face-down card to turn over—turn over the top card of the next-highest card pile.

To win the game: Get all the cards turned face up before the fourth King is turned face up.

Double or Quits

Other Names: None
Space: Small
Level: Easy

Tricky building—and on only one foundation!

Layout: Deal seven cards in a sort of frame shape, as shown below. Then place a card inside the frame. That card is the foundation, and you can build on it from the frame or from the stockpile. If any of the cards in the layout turn out to be Kings, put them on the bottom of the deck and replace them with other cards.

To win the game: Build all the cards onto the foundation—except for Kings—doubling the value of the card that has just been placed.

Play: For example, let's say the layout looks like this:

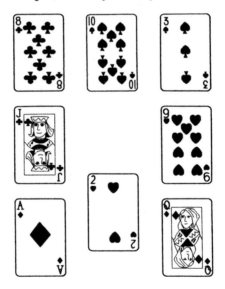

The card you've got to build on is a deuce, so you deal out the cards, one by one, until you come to a 4 of any suit—and place that on the deuce. The cards that you go through before you come to the 4 go on the wastepile.

The next card you need to find is double 4—or an 8. There is one in the frame, so you can use that right away. Spaces in the frame are filled with the top card of the wastepile or, if there is no wastepile, from your hand.

Double 8 is 16. So deduct 13 (the number of cards in a suit) and you get 3: This is the card you need to find next.

So—a sequence goes like this:

2 4 8 3 6 Queen (12) Jack (11) 9 5 10 7 A 2

and the sequence repeats.
Redeals: Two.

Duchess

Other Names: Glenwood
Space: Small
Level: Moderate

Layout: Lay out four fans of three cards each at the top of the table. Leave a space for the foundations, and then deal out a row of four cards.

To win the game: Build the four foundation cards into full 13-card suites.

Play: Choose any one of the exposed cards in the fans to be your foundation. For example, in the illustration above, it might make sense to choose the 3 of Diamonds as your foundation, because the 3 of Spades is available to build onto the foundation and so is the 4 of Diamonds.

After you make all possible moves to the foundations, you can start building downward on the row of cards, in alternating colors. You are allowed to move all the cards of one pile onto another pile as a unit, when the cards are in the correct sequence (down by suit).

Go through the stockpile of cards, one by one, building to the foundations or the layout—or discarding the unplayable cards to the wastepile.

When spaces open up in the row, fill them from the fans—and when no fans are left, from the wastepile.

Redeal: One.

Eagle Wing

Other Names: Thirteen Down
Wings
Space: Moderate
Level: Difficult

Layout: Deal 13 cards and place them face down in a pile in the middle of the table. This pile is known as "the trunk." Then lay out four cards, face up, on one side of the pile, and four cards face up on the other. These are the "wings" of the eagle.

Deal out one more card and place it directly above the pile, so that your layout looks like this:

That last card is a foundation pile. As other 8s appear, they go up in a row alongside it and you build on them as well.

To win the game: Build the foundations up to full 13-card suites.

Play: Go through the cards, one by one. If you cannot play a card onto one of the foundation piles, put it in a wastepile. The top of the wastepile is always available for play.

You can also build with the cards in the wings. When a space opens up in the wings, fill it right away with a card from the trunk. The bottom card in the trunk—if you get that far—may be played directly to the foundation without waiting for a place in the wings.

In the building, Aces follow Kings.

Redeals: You are allowed two (three times through the cards).

Fortress

Other Names: Fort
Space: Large
Level: Difficult

Layout: Deal out five columns of five cards each on both sides of the playing space. Lay out the entire deck, face up, adding an extra card to the top rows.

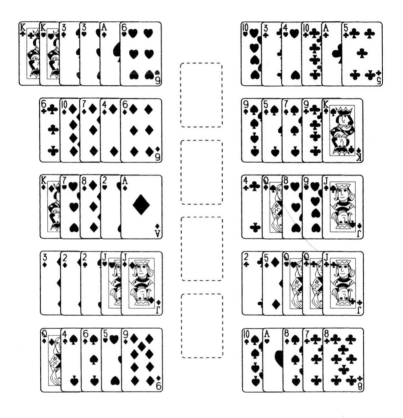

Foundations—Aces, as they become available—are placed in the middle column, as in the illustration.
To win the game: Build up the Aces in suit to Kings.

Play: After playing whatever cards you can to the foundations, you can start building in suit on the exposed cards in the layout, one card at a time. You can build up or down on the layout, but not both ways in the same row.

Chessboard

Other Names: Fives

Play in exactly the same way as *Fortress*, except instead of putting Aces in the foundation column, choose whatever card you want after dealing out the layout.

Fourteens

Other Names: Fourteen Puzzle
Fourteen Out
Take Fourteen

Space: Large
Level: Easy

Layout: Deal the cards, face up, in 12 columns of four cards each. You'll have four cards left over. Just put them on the first four columns.

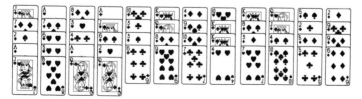

Arrange the cards so that you can see them all.

Play: Remove pairs of available cards whose totals add up to 14. There will be, of course:

Ace and King	4 and 10
2 and Queen	5 and 9
3 and Jack	6 and 8

Available cards are the ones that are exposed at the bottoms of the columns.

To win the game: You win when all the cards have been discarded.

Gaps

Other Names: Spaces
Space: Large
Level: Difficult

Layout: Deal all the cards in the pack—in four rows of 13 cards, each face up.

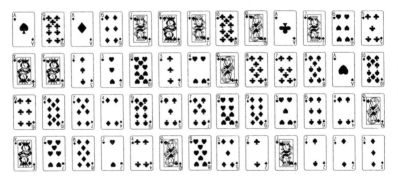

Then remove the Aces. This leaves gaps in the layout. These gaps must be filled by the card that is next higher in rank to the card on the left—and in the same suit. For example, suppose the gap opens up to the right of a 3 of Hearts. It must be filled by a 4 of Hearts.

If the gap opens up in the first space at the left of a row, it may be filled with any deuce.

If the gap opens up after a King, it cannot be filled. Action is blocked.

When a King blocks the action in every row, the deal is over.

To win the game: Get each row into a sequence of cards from 2 to King, by suit.

Redeals: As many as you want. You need to gather up the cards in a special way for the redeal. Leave in place the deuces that appear at the left end of a row and any cards that follow it in the correct sequence and suit. For example:

leave these   **but not these**

Then, gather up all the not-in-place cards, shuffle them, and deal them out as follows:

1. Leave one gap to the right of each sequence.
2. If the only card in place is a 2, leave a gap to the right of it.
3. If there is no 2 in the row, leave a gap at the start of the row, so that a 2 can be moved in.

The Garden

Other Names: Flower Garden
Parterre
Bouquet

Space: Large
Level: Easy

Layout: Deal six columns of six overlapping cards. This is "the garden."

Spread the remaining cards out in front of you. They are "the bouquet." The layout looks like this:

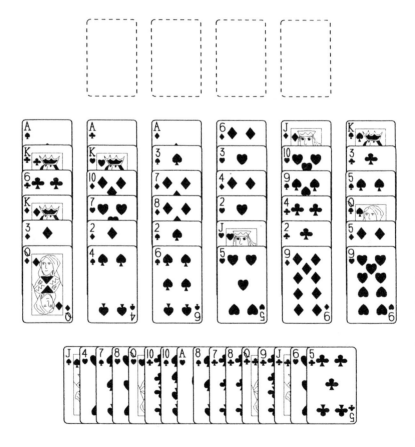

The cards spread out at the bottom are available to play onto the layout, building down one by one regardless of suit.

As the foundations—the Aces—become available, they are placed above the layout.

To win the game: Build the Aces up in suit to Kings.

Play: Start building on the exposed cards at the bottom of the columns, one card at a time, and to the foundations. If a complete column is cleared away, the space may be filled by any available card. Every card of the bouquet is available for building at all times.

Golf

Other Names: None
Space: Moderate
Level: Difficult

Layout: Deal seven rows of five cards each, so that the layout looks like this:

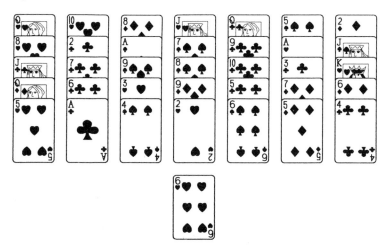

Deal one card below that will start the wastepile.

To win the game: Get rid of the entire layout by building up and down on the wastepile, regardless of suit.

Play: Only the exposed cards of the layout are available for building. In the example above, the 5 of Hearts can go on the wastepile; the 4 of Spades can go on that, opening the way for the 3 of Hearts. Then you can go in the other direction with the 4 of Clubs, and so on.

You can't build anything on a King. When you put a King on the wastepile, you've ended the sequence. Whenever you end a sequence—by putting down a King or not being able to make another move—you can take a card from the stockpile of 17 cards that never got into the layout. Place the card on the wastepile and resume play. If you use up all the cards in the deck, and still have cards in the layout, you've lost the game.

Grandfather's Clock

Other Names: **None**
Space: **Huge**
Level: **Easy**

Layout: Remove the following cards from the deck and place them in a circle, as in the illustration below:

2 of Hearts	8 of Diamonds
3 of Spades	9 of Clubs
4 of Diamonds	10 of Hearts
5 of Clubs	Jack of Spades
6 of Hearts	Queen of Diamonds
7 of Spades	King of Clubs

These are the
foundations
on which you are
going to be building
a "real" clock face.

Place the remaining cards in eight columns of five cards each.

Overlap the cards so you can see them all.

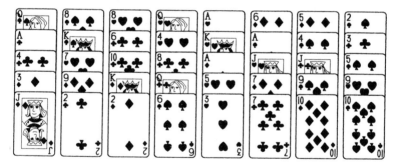

Play: Using the exposed cards in the layout, build the foundations—the cards on the clock face—up in suit until the cards on the top correspond to the numbers on a real clock face (with Jack as 11 o'clock and the Queen at 12).

In order to free the cards to do this, build on the cards

in the layout—downward, regardless of suit.

Spaces may be filled by any available card.

To win the game: Get the clock to have the right number values on its face, as in the illustration below:

Hit or Miss

Other Names:	**Treize**	**Roll Call**
	Talkative	**Harvest**

Space: Small
Level: Very Difficult

Play: Go through the cards one by one, naming each one as you go. The first one would be "Ace," the second "Deuce," the eleventh "Jack," and so on.

When your name and the rank of the card are the same, it's a *hit*, and you get to discard the card.

You are allowed to go through the cards as many times as you want—or until you go through the entire pack twice without a hit.

To win the game: Discard every card in the deck.

King Albert

Other Names: Idiot's Delight
Space: Large
Level: Easy

Layout: Deal a row of nine cards face up. Then deal a row of eight cards face up on top of them, leaving the first card uncovered. Continue placing rows of cards, each one card less than the row before, leaving the first card uncovered.

You'll have seven cards left when you finish laying out the cards. These are "free" cards, which you can use any way you want—on the layout or the foundations.

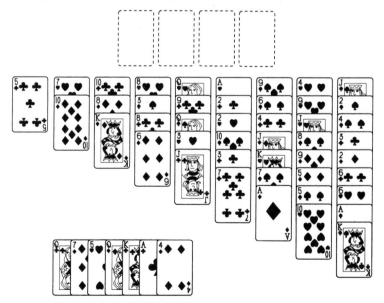

To win the game: Release the Aces and build them up to Kings in suit.

Play: Once the cards are laid out, play whatever you can to the foundations, which you set up above the layout. Then build on the layout itself—downward in alternating colors.

Only one card at a time may be built on the foundations or the layout.

A space may be filled by any available card.

Klondike

Other Names: **Canfield**   **Small Triangle**
                   Fascination **Demon Patience**
                   Triangle
Space: Moderate
Level: Difficult

Layout: Lay out seven cards in a row—face down except for the first card. Then put the eighth card face up on the second card in the row, and complete the row with face-down cards. Place a face-up card on the third pile, and finish off the row in the same way. Continue until you have a face-up card on every pile.

Your layout will look like this:

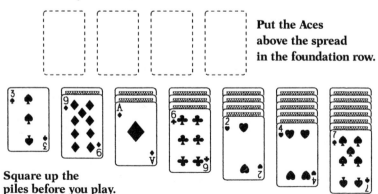

Put the Aces above the spread in the foundation row.

Square up the piles before you play.

Aces are low in this game.

To win the game: Build up complete suites from Ace to King.

Play: First, look over the spread carefully. Move any cards that you can to the foundation row—Aces and any cards you can build on them.

You can also build cards on the layout itself. Only the face-up cards are available for this building, and only if they are the exposed cards of the pile. Then you can build downward in alternating colors.

In the example, shown here, you can move the Ace to the foundation row, and then move the black 3 onto the red 4, and the red 2 onto the black 3.

Every time you move a face-up card, you need to turn up the face-down card beneath it. When there are no more face-down cards in a pile, you have a space. Spaces can be filled by any available King.

When you've made all the moves you can, start going through the stockpile one by one, looking for more cards to build onto the foundations and the layout. If you can't place the card, it goes face up onto a wastepile, and the top card of the wastepile is available for play.

Scoring: Five rounds make a game. Add up the number of foundation cards you've come up with in each round for your final score.

Klondike by Threes _____

This game is played exactly the same as *Klondike*, but you go through the stockpile of cards by threes. Because of that, you get redeals. Rules vary about how many redeals you get. Some say two (three trips through the cards), and some say as many as you want.

Redeals: Two (or more).

Agnes

Space: Moderate
Level: Moderate

Play exactly the same way as *Klondike*, except:

1. When you finish the layout, deal the next card above it to make the first foundation. Aces, of course, need to be played between the Kings and 2s.

2. Below the layout, deal a row of seven cards. These are available to be played onto the layout and the foundations. Play as many of them as you like, and when you have no more moves to make, deal another seven cards on top of them. You'll probably have spaces in that row of seven; be sure not to skip them when you deal the second row. After you deal a third layer of seven cards, you'll have two cards left in your hand. Turn them face up. They are available too.

3. Spaces in the layout may be filled by any card that is one lower than the foundation card. For example, if the foundation card is a 2, the spaces can be filled only with Aces.

Whitehead

Level: Moderate/Difficult

Play exactly the same as *Klondike*, except:

1. Deal all the cards face up.

2. Instead of building in alternate colors, build red on red, black on black.

3. When spaces open up in the layout, fill them with any available card or group of cards.

4. When moving piles of cards as a unit, you may do it only where the cards are in sequence by suit.

Thumb and Pouch

Level: Easy

Play exactly the same way as *Klondike*, except:
1. When building, a card can be laid on any card that is one rank higher regardless of color—except one of its own suit.
2. A space may be filled by any available card or sequence of cards.

La Belle Lucie

Other Names:
   The Fan   **Clover Leaf**
   Alexander the Great   **Midnight Oil**
   Three Shuffles and   **Fair Lucy**
      a Draw

Space: Large
Level: Moderate

This is one of the most delightful solitaire games.

Layout: Lay out the whole deck in sets of three, face up.

One single card will be left over, which becomes a set of its own.

     The only cards that may be moved are the exposed ones on top of the sets. They are built up on the foundations or on the top cards of other sets, by suit, building downward.

To win the game: Release the Aces and build them up in suit to Kings.

Play: Once you have the cards laid out, move the Aces that are available onto the foundations. In the example above, the Ace of Hearts is available for one of the foundations; so are the 2 and 3 of Hearts. Then proceed to build on the top cards of the fans, one card at a time. When a fan is entirely eliminated, it is not replaced.

Redeals: Two. To redeal, gather up the fans, shuffle the cards, and set down in groups of three as before. Any left-over cards are sets by themselves.

Special bonus: In the last redeal, when you're stuck, you get one free move—one card you can pull from underneath one or two others and play in any way you want.

Super Flower Garden

Level: Easy

Play exactly the same way as *La Belle Lucie*, except building takes place regardless of suit.

Trefoil

Other Names: Les Fleurons

Play exactly the same way as *La Belle Lucie*, except you put the Aces in a foundation row before laying out the fans. You'll then have 16 complete fans.

Shamrocks

Other Names: Three-card Fan
Level: Easy

Play exactly the same way as *La Belle Lucie*, except:
1. If a King is on the top of a set and a card of lower rank in the same suit lies under it, you can put the King under that card.
2. No fan may contain more than three cards.

Little Spider

Other Names: None
Space: Small
Level: Moderate

Layout: Lay out four cards face up in a row along the top of your playing space, and four cards in a row beneath them—leaving space for a row in between. That's where the foundations will go—two Aces of one color and two Kings of another—as they become available:

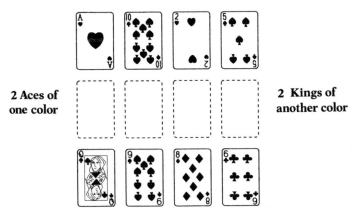

2 Aces of one color

2 Kings of another color

To win the game: Build the Aces in suit to Kings and the Kings in suit to Aces.

During the deal: You can move any card from the top row onto the foundations. But you cannot move a card from the bottom row unless it can be moved straight up into place—into the position directly above its original position. For example, in the illustration on the left on page 53, the 2 of Hearts can go on the Ace of Hearts, but in the picture on the right, it can't.

Play: When you've made all the moves you can to the foundations, deal another four cards to the top and bottom rows. Make your moves, and then deal again—until all the cards have been laid out.

At this point, the special rules that for "During the deal" no longer apply. You can move any card from the top or bottom rows onto the foundation piles. You can also build top cards from the layout onto each other regardless of suit or color—up or down.

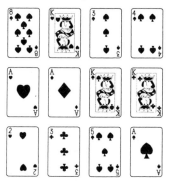

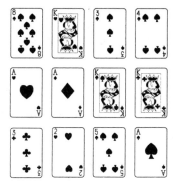

2 of Hearts can go straight up onto the Ace, because the Ace is the same suit.

2 of Hearts cannot go onto the Ace, because it is not directly under the Ace of Hearts.

Spaces in the layout may not be filled.
Kings may be placed on Aces.

Monte Carlo

Other Names: Weddings
Space: Moderate
Level: Moderate

Layout: Deal five rows of five cards each, so your layout looks like this:

To win the game: Discard the entire deck in pairs of the same rank. You can discard them if they are:
1. Next to each other
2. Above or below each other
3. "Touching" diagonally

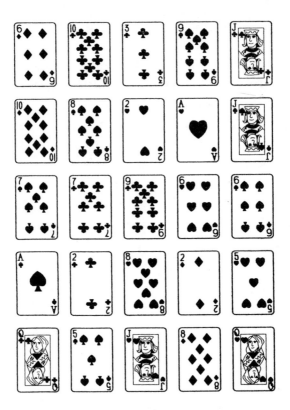

Play: Remove every pair that you can from the layout. When you do, there will be holes. Close up the cards so that all the holes are filled and the cards are in the same order in which you laid them out.

After you make the cards into solid rows again, deal new cards to make up the bottom rows, so that you have five rows of five cards again.

Remove the pairs again in the same way, and when you can't move any more cards, go through the process of closing up the spaces in the layout and filling in at the end with cards from your hand.

Nestor

Other Names: Matrimony
Space: Moderate
Level: Moderate

Layout: Deal eight cards face up in a row. Then deal another five rows overlapping them, so that you can see all the rows at one time.

As you deal, make sure you don't have any cards of the same rank in a column. If you're about to deal a deuce onto a column where a deuce already appears, slip the card underneath the pack and deal another card instead.

You'll have four cards left over when you finish dealing. They are the stock.

Play: Remove cards of the same rank by twos from the exposed cards at the ends of the columns. When you can't make any more moves, turn up the first card of the stockpile. If that won't help you, turn up the next, and the next.

To win the game: Discard the whole layout by twos.

Osmosis

Other Names: **Treasure Trove**
Space: **Small**
Level: **Moderate**

Layout: Deal four sets of four
cards each face down. Then
square them off face up and put
them in a column at the left side
of your playing space. Place the
next card in the deck (which
becomes the first foundation) to
the right of the top card.

Place additional foundation cards
(other cards of the same rank), as
they become available, in a
column under the first.

To win the game: Build each foundation card to a full 13
cards in suit but regardless of sequence.
Special building rule: No card may be placed in the
second, third, or fourth foundation rows unless a card of the
same rank has already been placed on the previous foundation card.
Play: Let's see how this works. In the illustration the foundation card is the 5 of Hearts. The first thing to do is to build
any other Hearts that are already showing on the table—
such as the 10 and the King—and put them alongside the 5,
overlapping, so you can see what cards have been played to
this foundation.

Then start going through the cards in the stockpile,
three at a time, to find additional Hearts and more foundation cards for the other suits.

Let's say you turn up a 5 of Clubs. You place it below the 5 of Hearts.

The next card you turn up is a Queen of Clubs. You cannot place it—because the only cards that have been placed in the Hearts row are the King and the 10. So those are the only Clubs you could put down beside the 5 of Clubs.

The next card you get is the 5 of Diamonds, and you place it under the 5 of Clubs.

And then you get a 10 of Diamonds. You cannot place it next to the 5 of Diamonds—even though there is a 10 of Hearts out on the table, because the 10 of Clubs has not yet been placed.

Redeals: You get to go through the cards until you win the game—or until the game is blocked.

Peek

Play exactly the same way as *Osmosis*, except with the face-down cards turned up and spread so that you can see them all.

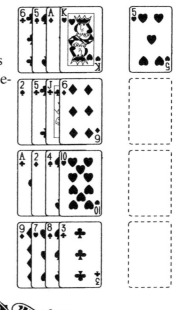

Poker Solitaire

Other Names: Poker Squares
Space: Moderate
Level: Moderate

Layout: Deal 25 cards in five rows of five cards each. Each row and each column is a poker hand; so, in any game, you have ten hands with which to build your total score.

To win the game: Come up with the highest score.

Play: Rearrange the cards in the layout so that you have the highest-scoring poker hand possible.

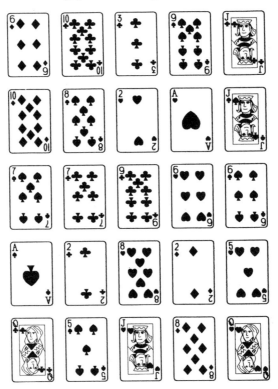

In some versions of this game, after you move a card once, you cannot move it again.

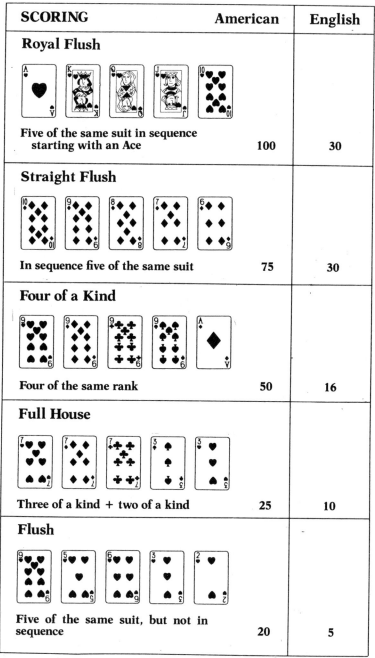

SCORING	American	English
Royal Flush Five of the same suit in sequence starting with an Ace	100	30
Straight Flush In sequence five of the same suit	75	30
Four of a Kind Four of the same rank	50	16
Full House Three of a kind + two of a kind	25	10
Flush Five of the same suit, but not in sequence	20	5

continued on the next page

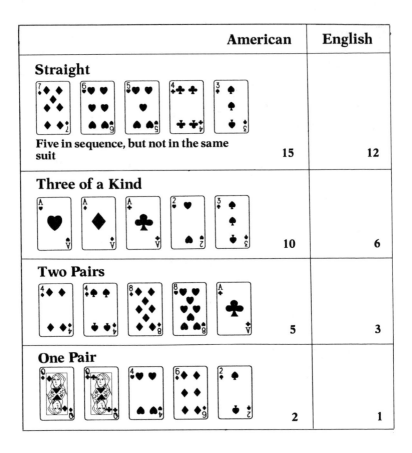

	American	English
Straight Five in sequence, but not in the same suit	15	12
Three of a Kind	10	6
Two Pairs	5	3
One Pair	2	1

Pyramid

Other Names: Pile of 28
Space: Moderate
Level: Difficult

A sad thing about many solitaire games is that you play a round—or five rounds—and then it's over. You have no special feeling of victory (unless you've played out and won) and no standard with which to compare your score.

Here's a game that keeps you counting and scoring all the time. You can play it against yourself, against another player, or against "par."

Layout: Lay out the cards in the shape of a pyramid, starting with one card at the top and placing two cards that overlap it, then three overlapping them, and so on, until you have a large triangle with seven cards at its base.

Each card has its own numerical value (face value); Kings count as 13, Queens as 12, and Jacks as 11.

Play: Your job is to remove pairs of cards that add up to 13, with this catch: You cannot remove a card unless it is "exposed"—not covered by any other card.

For example, in the pyramid above, you can remove the 7 and the 6 from the bottom row. This opens up the Ace in the row above, which you can remove with the Queen (worth 12) in the bottom row.

You can remove Kings alone, because they add up to 13 without any help.

Place all the cards you remove in a special "Removed" pile, face up. The top card in this pile can be used again to form another 13-match.

Now you start dealing out the rest of the pack, one by

one. If the card you turn up does not form a match with an available card in the pyramid, put it into a wastepile. Don't mix up this pile with your "Removed" pile.

If one of the cards you turn up from your hand is a match with the top card of the "Removed" pile, you can remove both of them.

To win the game: You need to remove the entire pyramid plus the cards in your hand.

Redeals: Two.

HOW TO SCORE PYRAMID

A match is six games. Score each game as follows:

50 points—If you get rid of your pyramid in the first deal (once through all the cards in the deck).

50 points minus—If you get rid of the pyramid during the first deal but still have cards in your hand or in the wastepile, score 50 points minus the number of cards in the wastepile.

35 points minus—If you get rid of the pyramid during the second deal, but still have cards in your hand or in the wastepile, score 35 points minus the number of cards in your hand and the wastepile.

20 points minus—If you get rid of the pyramid during the third deal, score 20 points minus the number of cards in your hand or the wastepile.

0 points minus—If you never do succeed in getting rid of your pyramid, deduct one point for each card left in the pyramid as well as each card left in your hand and the wastepile. That's right—a minus score!

"Par" is 0 for six matches. If you do better, you've won!

Quadrille

Other Names: Captive Queens
La Française
Partners

Space: Moderate

Level: Easy

Layout: The layout for this game is set up as you play. The design that is to be created appears below:

Play: Start turning up cards from the deck. As soon as the 5s and 6s appear, put them in place and start building on them. On the 5s you build down: **4 3 2 Ace King**.

On the 6s you build up: **7 8 9 10 Jack**.

The Queens just sit in the middle and look regal.

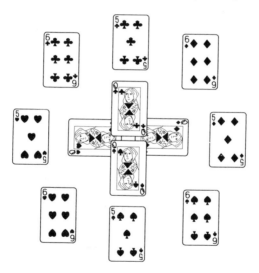

To win the game: Build the 6s up in suit to the Jacks and the 5s down in suit to the Kings.

Redeals: Two.

Queen's Audience

Other Names: King's Audience
Space: Moderate
Level: Easy

Layout: Make a square of four cards to a side, like this:

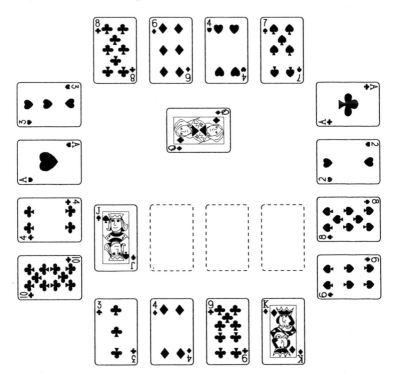

This is the Queen's antechamber. The space inside it is the Queen's Audience. Into the Audience will go the Jacks, as they appear. They are the foundations.

To win the game: Build the foundations from Jack to deuce in suit.

Special building rule: Before a Jack can get into the Queen's Audience, an Ace of the same suit has to go with him. That Ace can come from the walls of the antechamber or from the stockpile. Put the Ace under the Jack.

Kings and Queens get to come into the Audience also, but only in pairs of the same suit. Put the King under the Queen.

Play: Go through the cards one by one, building to the foundations and discarding Queen and King sets into the Audience.

Spaces in the antechamber wall should be filled right away from the top card of the wastepile or the stockpile.

Russian Solitaire

Other Names: None
Space: Large
Level: Very Difficult

Some people say this is the most difficult solitaire game in the world to win. In any case, it is one of the most intriguing.

Layout: Lay out the cards exactly as you lay them out for *Klondike*, but when you finish, deal the rest of the pack face up on top of the layout, as in the illustration on page 66.

To win the game: Free the Aces from the layout and build them up to Kings in suit in a row above the layout.

Play: First, move any Aces that are exposed onto the foundations. Then build downward in suit on the exposed cards of the layout. In order to do this, you will often have to move more than one card at a time—sometimes as many as a whole column of unrelated cards.

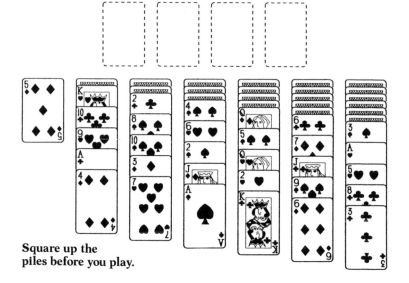

Square up the piles before you play.

In the layout below, for example:

First, you would move the Ace up to the foundation row, just as in *Klondike*. Then, you would start looking at the other cards that are exposed. The 6 of Diamonds is lying open. You could put the 5 of Diamonds on it, thereby creating a space in the layout. That vacant spot, just as in *Klondike*, can be filled with any King. Suppose you decided to move the King of Hearts. You would have to move the entire column of cards on top of the King to the #1 space. There is only one card underneath the King. Turn it over: it's the King of Diamonds. And it is now the leading card of the second column.

Your next move might be to put the 4 of Diamonds on the 5 of Diamonds. That would open up the Ace of Clubs, which you can put up at the top in the foundation row.

You might then move the 6 of Hearts down onto the 7. Remember that when you move the 6, all the cards on top of it must move too.

Now your layout would look pretty crazy, like the illustration on page 67.

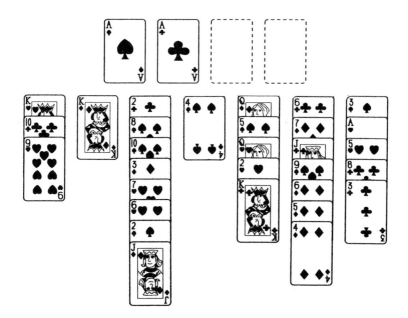

Well, you get the idea.

Play five rounds of this game, adding up the number of points in each for your total score.

Yukon

Level: Moderate

Play in exactly the same way as *Russian Solitaire*, except building on the bottom cards of the layout is done regardless of suit in alternating colors.

Scorpion

Other Names: None
Space: Large
Level: Moderate

Layout: Deal a row of seven cards—four face down and three face up. Repeat this same pattern in a second and third row, overlapping the cards each time. Then deal out all the rest of the cards face up on top of this beginning setup. You'll have three cards left over at the end. Put them aside for a few minutes. Your layout will look like this:

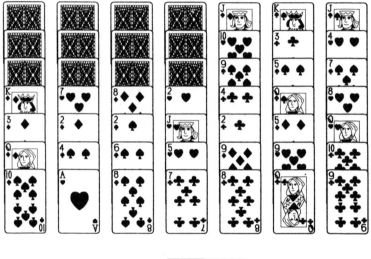

Play: Now you are going to build downward in suit on the exposed cards of the layout. But you are not limited to moving one card at a time. You may move any card that meets the requirements of rank and suit—even if it is covered with cards. You just move all the cards with it.

As columns are emptied, you can fill them with Kings—along with the cards that are on top of them.

Nothing can be built on an Ace.

When you have exhausted all chances for moves, take the three cards you set aside at the start and place one on each of the bottom cards of the left-hand columns. That picks up the game and can give you a few new moves.

To win the game: Build four Kings, right on the layout, with their full suites, like this:

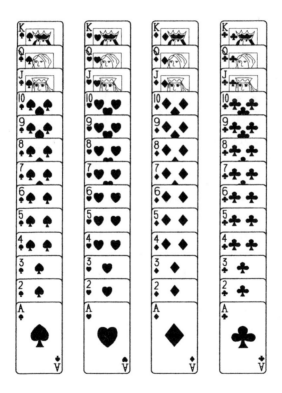

Spiderette

Other Names: None
Space: Moderate
Level: Difficult

When you're tired and angry at playing *Klondike* and never playing out, you might want to get even with this Cheater's version.

Layout: Lay out the cards the same way you would for *Klondike*, but this time, you're not going to set up any foundation piles.

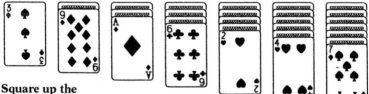

Square up the piles before you play.

Play: Build downward on the layout, regardless of suits and colors (but try to build in suit where you can). You can move groups of cards when they are in the correct sequence. When a space opens up in the layout, you can fill it with any available card or sequence of cards.

Whenever you run out of moves to make, deal another seven cards on the layout. At the end, put the last three cards on the first three columns.

When you get all 13 cards of one suit in order in one pile, you can discard them.

To win the game: Build up and then discard all four complete suits.

Vanishing Cross

Other Names: **Corner Card**   **Four Seasons**
                     Corners   **Czarina**

Space: **Small**
Level: **Moderate**

Layout: Place five cards on the table in the shape of a cross. This is the layout. Then place another card in the upper left-hand corner. That is the foundation. The other foundations—the same rank as the corner card—should be placed in the other corners as they become available.

foundation   →

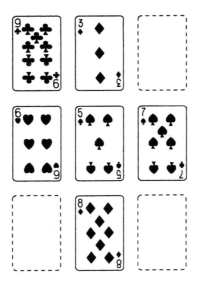

Play: Build whatever cards you can onto the foundation, upward in suit. Then build whatever cards you can onto others in the cross—downward and regardless of suit. When you've exhausted all the possibilities, start going through the stockpile, one card at a time, playing it to the foundation (going up), to the cards in the cross (going down), or, if unplayable, to a wastepile.

To win the game: Build all the corner cards into four suites.

Note: Aces may be placed on Kings.

Two-Pack Games

British Square

Other Names: None
Space: Moderate
Level: Easy

Layout: Deal four rows of four cards each, face up. Four Aces, one of each suit, as they become available, will be placed above the layout as foundations.

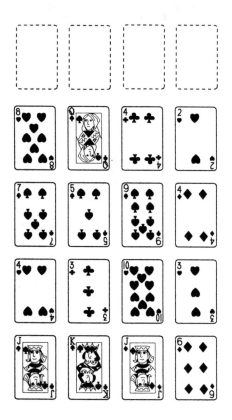

To win the game: Build the Aces up to Kings in suit—and here's the tricky part—then place another King of the same suit on top of that King and build down in suit to Aces.
Play: Besides building on the foundations, you also build

on the layout, up or down in suit. You can build in either direction, but once you decide on a particular direction for any given pile, you have to keep it that way for the entire game.

When you've made all the moves you can make in the layout and to the foundations, start turning over one card at a time to play to the foundations, the layout, or to a wastepile.

You may fill spaces from the top card of the wastepile or from your hand.

Busy Aces

Other Names: None
Space: Small
Level: Easy

Layout: Deal two rows of six cards each, face up. Aces, as they become available, are foundations and are placed in a row above.

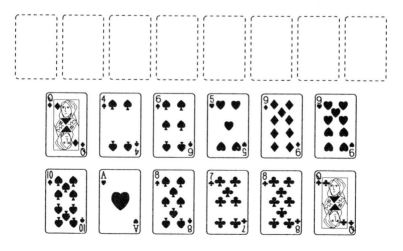

Play: Do whatever building you can at the start on the foundations. Then, build on the layout, downward and in suit. After you've made all the moves you can, begin turning over cards one by one, discarding unplayable cards onto a wastepile.

When spaces open up in the layout, fill them from your hand or the wastepile.

To win the game: Build all eight Aces up in suit to Kings.

Capricieuse

Other Names: None
Space: Moderate
Level: Easy

Layout: Select one Ace and one King of each suit, and place them in a single line.

Then deal out the rest of the pack in 12 face-up piles.

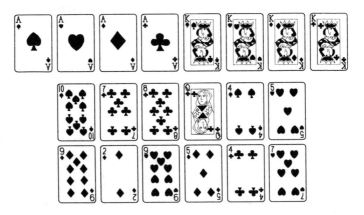

Play: As you deal the cards onto the piles, play any appropriate card from your hand onto the foundations. *Only* cards from your hand can go onto the foundations during the deal—be sure not to move any from the layout.

Don't leave any blanks in the layout as you deal—give a card to each pile. If one card can be played onto the foundation, substitute another card for it in the layout.

When all the cards have been dealt, start building them on each other, in suit.

Kings may not be put on Aces, nor Aces on Kings.

Redeals: Two. When gathering up the cards for a redeal, pick them up in reverse sequence from the way you dealt them.

Congress

Other Names: President's Cabinet
Space: Small
Level: Difficult

Layout: Deal a column of four cards to the left and a column of four to the right. Leave enough space between them for the foundations, eight Aces.

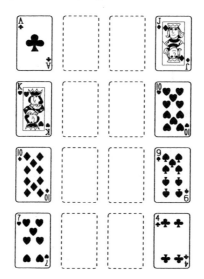

To win the game: Build the Aces upward in suit to Kings.
Play: First, make whatever moves you can to the foundations. Then, start turning over the cards in your hand one by one, building downward on the layout, regardless of suit, and playing whatever cards you can to the foundations. Fill in spaces from the wastepile or from your hand. Any card on top of a pile is available for building.

Cotillion

Other Names: Contradance
Space: Small
Level: Moderate

Layout: Select one 5 of every suit and one 6 of every suit. These are the foundations. Set them up like this:

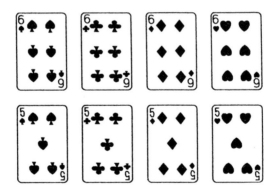

Play: Go through the balance of the cards one by one and play them to the foundations in suit wherever you can.
To win the game: Build the 6s up to Queens and the 5s down (through Aces) to Kings.
Redeals: One.

Crescent

Other Names: None
Space: Large
Level: Moderate

Layout: Select one Ace and one King from each suit and place them in two rows, Kings on top.

Then deal the rest of the cards in a semicircle around them in 16 piles. Put the first five cards face down, the top card face up.

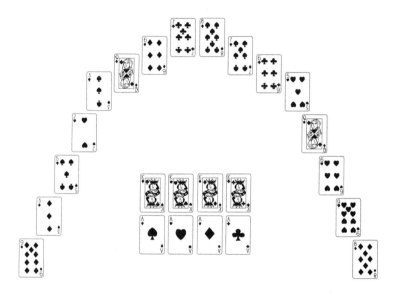

To win the game: Build Aces up to Kings in suit and Kings down to Aces in suit.

Play: Play whatever cards you can to the foundations. Then you can start building up or down on the layout in suit. When you move the top card of a pile, turn up the card underneath.

When you use up all the cards in a pile and you have an empty space, it cannot be refilled.

Shifting: When you can't make any more moves, take the

bottom card from each pile and place it on top of the pile, face up. You need to do this with every pile before you stop to make any moves. You can make this unusual shifting move three times during the game; it's a little like having three redeals.

Reverse: When the top cards of two foundations of the same suit are in sequence, you can transfer one or more cards from one foundation to the other. The original Ace and King may not be transferred.

Open Crescent

Play exactly the same as *Crescent*, but lay out the cards face up and spread them so that you can see them as you play.

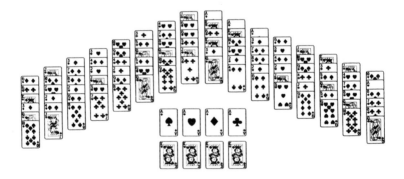

It's a more interesting game when strategy comes into play.

Diplomat

Other Names: None
Space: Moderate
Level: Easy

Similar to the one-pack *Streets and Alleys*, this game is fairly quick to set up and has lots of action.

Layout: Deal four columns of four overlapping cards, leaving space between them for two columns of side-by-side Aces, which are the foundations as they become available.

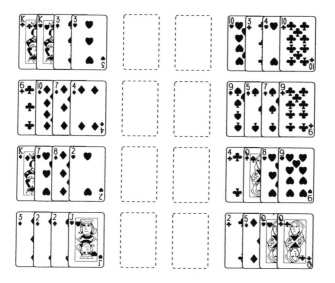

To win the game: Build the Aces up in suit to Kings.

Play: After making whatever moves you can to the foundations, you build downward on the exposed cards of the layout, regardless of suit.

When you can't make any more moves, start turning over the cards in your hand, one by one, playing what you can to the layout. Place the unused cards in a wastepile. The top card of the wastepile, the card in your hand, and the exposed cards in the layout are all available to play onto foundations, onto the layout, and to fill any spaces that open up in the layout.

Redeals: One. Just turn over the wastepile.

The Fan

Other Names: None
Space: Wide
Level: Easy/Moderate

Layout: First, count out 12 cards in one unit. This is the stockpile. Place it face up at the left. Beside it, place an overlapping string of 12 face-up cards. The next card in your hand will be a foundation card. Let's say it's the 10 of Clubs. Leave space next to it for placing the other 10s—seven more of them, as they become available. They will be foundation cards on which you build up from 10s through Aces to 9s.

Underneath this foundation row, deal out four cards from the pack, face up.

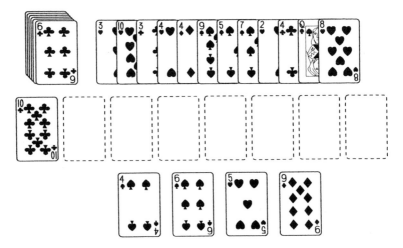

To win the game: All foundations are to be built in se-quence, regardless of suits, until they contain 13 cards. But whether you build upward or downward is up to you. You can make up your mind after you see how the game is shaping up. You don't have to decide until you're ready to start building, but whatever you decide, it will apply to all the foundations.

Play: Start playing onto the foundations by going through the cards in your hand—one by one. Unplayable cards go into a wastepile.

You can also play onto the foundations with the follow-ing cards:

1. the top card of the stockpile
2. the exposed card on the end of the string of overlapping cards
3. the four-card row
4. the top card of the wastepile

If a space opens up in the row of four cards, fill it from the wastepile or the cards in your hand.

Redeals: You get two redeals (that means going through the cards three times).

Forty Thieves

Other Names: Big Forty   Cadran
                 Napoleon at   Roosevelt at
                    St. Helena   San Juan

Space: Large
Level: Moderate

Layout: Deal four rows of ten cards each, overlapping, as in the picture. Aces, as they become available, are moved up above the layout as foundations.

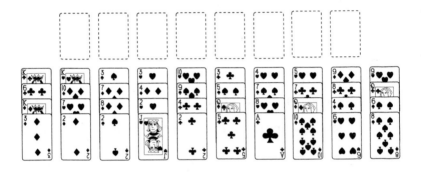

To win the game: Build all eight Aces to Kings in suit.

Play: First, build what you can to the foundations. Then build on the layout itself, downward in suit. For example, in the illustration above, the 2 of Diamonds can be placed on the 3 of Diamonds. The Ace of Clubs can be played up to the foundation row. So can the 2. When you have exhausted all the possibilities, start going through the cards one by one, building onto foundations or layout or discarding the unplayable cards into a wastepile. The top card of that wastepile is available too.

When a space opens up in the layout, you can fill it with any card—one from the layout, the top card from the wastepile, or a card from your hand.

Streets

Space: Large
Level: Moderate

Play exactly the same as *Forty Thieves*, except build downward on the layout in alternating colors.

Indian

Space: Large
Level: Easy

Play exactly the same as *Forty Thieves*, except:
1. For the layout, deal 30 cards in three rows of ten cards each. The first row should be face down.
2. When building on the layout, cards may go on any suit *except* their own.

Rank and File

Other Names: Dress Parade
　　　　　　　　Deauville
　　　　　　　　Emperor
Space: Large
Level: Moderate

Play exactly the same as *Forty Thieves*, except:
1. For the layout, deal the first three rows face down.
2. Build downward on the layout in alternating colors.
3. When all the cards on the top of a pile are in correct sequence, you're allowed to move them as a unit onto another pile in the layout.

Lucas

Space: Large
Level: Easy

Play exactly the same as *Forty Thieves*, except:
1. Set up the Aces in the foundation row before dealing the layout.
2. For the layout, deal three rows of 13 cards each. This makes for a much easier game.

Maria

Space: Large
Level: Moderate

Play exactly the same as *Forty Thieves*, except:
1. For the layout, deal four rows of nine cards each.
2. Build downward on the layout in alternating colors.

Number Ten

Space: Large
Level: Moderate

Play exactly the same as *Forty Thieves*, except:
1. Place the first two rows face down.
2. Build downward on the layout in alternating colors.
3. When all the cards on the top of a pile are in correct sequence, you're allowed to move them as a unit onto another pile in the layout.

Frog

Other Names: Toad
Toad-in-the-Hole
Space: Moderate
Level: Easy/Moderate

Layout: Count out 13 cards and place them in one pile face up. Make sure no Aces are within the pile. If there are any, replace them with other cards.

Then place one Ace next to the pack as a foundation. As other Aces appear, they should be placed next to it.

To win the game: Build all the Aces up by suit to Kings.
Play: Go through the stockpile, card by card. When cards are unplayable, place them in a row of their own underneath the foundation row—a row of five piles. You can put the cards in any positions you choose—all in one pile, if you want.

Fanny

Level: Moderate

Play exactly the same as *Frog*, except:
1. Count out only 12 cards instead of 13 for the face-up pile.
2. Do not set up an Ace to start the foundation row.

Grand Duchess

Other Names: Duchess of Luynes
Space: Small
Level: Moderate

Layout: Deal four cards in a row face up and an additional two cards face down to the side. Above them you'll be placing two rows of foundations, Aces (one of each suit) and Kings (one of each suit), as they become available.

To win the game: Build the Aces up in suit to Kings and the Kings down in suit to Aces.
Play: Make any possible moves and then deal again—four cards on top of the cards you dealt before and two more cards face down to the side. Make your moves and continue in this fashion, until you've gone through the entire pack.

Then turn up the face-down cards, spreading them out and playing any cards you can to the foundations and making whatever moves are possible.

Redeals: Three (four times through the cards). When you get ready to redeal, pick up the piles in reverse order, so that the pile at the right is on the top. Put the face-down pile at the bottom.

The first two redeals are done just as before, spreading out the face-down pile at the end. The last one is different; don't deal any cards face down to the side. Just deal the four cards onto the layout. Don't build up a face-down pile at all.

Parisienne

Play exactly the same as *Grand Duchess*, except lay out the Aces and Kings at the start.

The Harp

Other Names: **Klondike with two packs of cards**
Space: **Large**
Level: **Easy**

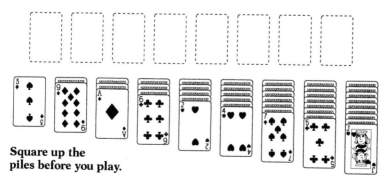

Square up the
piles before you play.

Play exactly the same as *Klondike*, except:

1. Use two packs of cards.
2. Use a nine-card row instead of a seven-card row.
3. There is no limit to the number of times you can go through the cards, one by one. Do it until you win or until the game is obviously blocked.
4. When filling a space, you may use an available King, as in *Klondike*, or you may use a group of cards in correct sequence that has a King at the top.

House in the Wood

Other Names: **Double Fan**
Space: **Large**
Level: **Easy**

This is a two-pack version of *La Belle Lucie*. But it works out much more often.

Layout: Lay out 34 fans of three cards each, plus one fan of two cards. The top cards of each fan are available for building onto foundations or onto other top cards.

To win the game: Free Aces from the fans and build them up in suit to Kings.

Play: After making all initial moves, start building on the exposed cards in the fans—up or down, but always in suit.

Spaces created by clearing away a fan are not filled.

Kings may not be put on Aces, nor Aces on Kings.

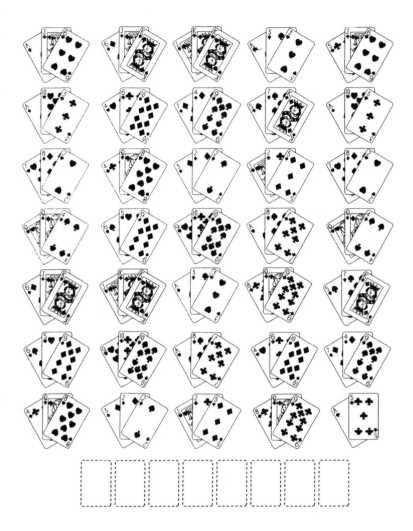

House on the Hill _____

Play exactly the same as *House in the Wood*, except instead of eight Aces as foundations, lay out one Ace and one King of each suit. Build the Aces up in suit to Kings and the Kings down to Aces.

Intelligence

Other Names: None
Space: Moderate
Level: Moderate/Difficult

Similar to the one-pack *La Belle Lucie*, but tougher, this is an intriguing game where you need to be bold to get enough cards into play.

Layout: Deal 18 fans of three cards, keeping the rest of the cards in a stockpile. As you deal, if Aces appear, put them right on the foundations and replace each one with the next card.

To win the game: Build the eight Aces up in suit to Kings.
Play: Once you've moved all the cards you can to the foundations, you can start building on the exposed cards of the fan, as you would in *La Belle Lucie*, up or down, in suit. You may reverse direction on the same pile.

Each time you completely eliminate a fan, you may replace it with three new cards from your hand. That is the only way to get new cards into play.

Kings may not be put on Aces, nor Aces on Kings.
Redeals: Two. While redealing, you still have the chance to pull Aces out of the fans, replacing them with the next card from your hand.

Matrimony

Other Names: None
Space: Moderate
Level: Difficult

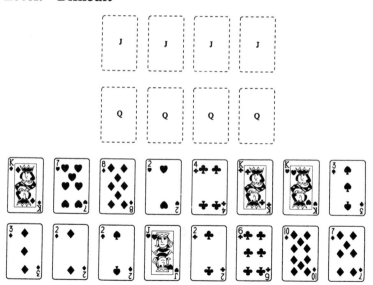

Layout: Lay out two rows of eight cards each. Then, as they become available, place four Queens of each suit and four Jacks of each suit above these rows, as foundations.

To win the game: Build the Queens upward in suit through Aces to Jacks, and the Jacks downward in suit through Aces to 10s.

Play: First, move any cards you can from the layout onto the foundations. Then deal 16 cards onto the layout—one on each card—or space (spaces are not filled except by this 16-card deal).

Make whatever moves you can and then, when you get stuck, deal another 16 cards onto the layout. The last deal will be only six cards, but deal it in the same way.

After you have used up all the cards in the deck and made all possible moves, pick up the pile in the lower right-hand corner, turn it face down, and deal the top card face up on its own place. Then continue dealing the pile, on each card in turn, starting at the upper left-hand corner.

Make any moves you can as a result of this play. Then, when you're stuck, pick up the 15th pile, turn it over, and deal that pile, first putting the top card in its own place and going on from there.

Again, make what moves you can. When you're stuck, pick up the next pile to the left and continue the process, until you've gone through all the piles once.

If you get stuck after dealing out pile #1, you've lost the game.

Miss Milligan

Other Names: None
Space: Moderate
Level: Difficult

To many, this is the ultimate solitaire game.

Layout: Deal out a row of eight cards. Move all Aces up above the row of cards, as they become available. The Aces are foundations.

To win the game: Build all eight Aces upward in suit to Kings.

Play: Besides building on the foundations, you also can build within the original row of eight cards—downward in alternating colors.

When you've made all possible moves, deal out another eight cards that overlap the original eight, filling in spaces as you go.

Play off what you can to the foundations, build what you can on the row, and deal another eight cards onto the layout.

Continue this process until you've used up all the cards in your hand. At this point you have the option of "weaving."

Weaving: This is the option of removing one card from the bottom row of the layout temporarily—while you make other moves. When you get that card back into play—either on a foundation or the layout—you are then allowed to remove another card. You can keep doing this until you win the game or until you can't find a place for the card.

Special rules: You are permitted to move two or more cards as a unit—when they are built correctly in rank and sequence and at the end of a column. For example, in the diagram below, you can move the 10 of Diamonds, 9 of Spades, and 8 of Hearts as a unit onto the Jack of Clubs.

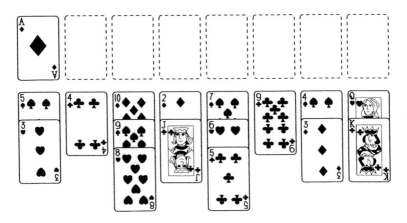

Spaces may be filled with any available King or with a sequence that leads off with a King.

Mount Olympus

Other Names: None
Space: Large/Moderate (for alternate layout)
Level: Easy

Layout: Remove all the Aces and deuces from the pack and set them out in an arch, alternating Aces and deuces, and colors, as in the picture.

All the Aces and deuces are foundations.

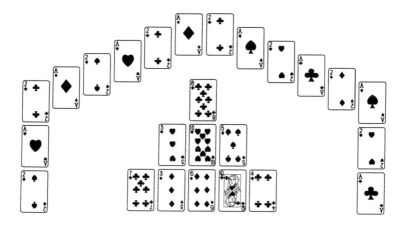

Then place nine cards in a pyramid shape beneath the arch.
To win the game: Build the foundations upward in suit by 2s: from Aces to Kings, deuces to Queens.

The Aces build like this: **A 3 5 7 9 J K**

The deuces build like this: **2 4 6 8 10 Q**

Play: You may also build on the cards in the pyramid in the same way—skipping a card as you go. Build them downward in suits.

When cards are in the correct rank and sequence, you can shift an entire pile as a unit.

When a space opens up in the pyramid, fill it at once with a card from the stockpile.

When you have made all possible moves and filled the spaces, deal nine more cards onto the pyramid. Make whatever plays you can onto the foundations, and then deal another nine cards. Continue this process until the stockpile is gone.

Note: If you don't have enough space to create the layout shown on page 97, you can set out the cards like this:

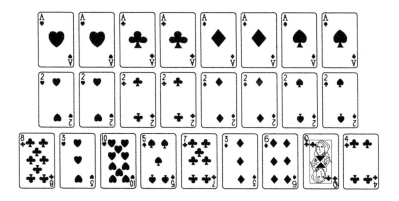

It is also an easier game to play in this format, because it is easier to build on the layout.

Napoleon's Square

Other Names: Quadruple Line
Space: Moderate
Level: Easy

Layout: Deal 12 piles of four cards each, four piles to the left (place them horizontally), four to the right (horizontally), and four across the top of the layout. All eight Aces will be placed in two rows in the middle of the layout as they become available.

To win the game: Build all the Aces upward in suit to Kings.

Play: First, make all the moves you can. Move Aces to the foundations and then build on the layout itself, downward

and in suit. The top card of any pile is available and so are groups of cards that are in sequence and in the same suit.

When a space opens up in the layout, fill it with any available card or group of cards in sequence and the same suit, or from your hand or from the wastepile.

After all initial moves have been made, turn over one card at a time from your hand, discarding unplayable cards to the wastepile. The top card of the wastepile is always available for play.

Odd and Even

Other Names: None
Space: Moderate
Level: Moderate

Layout: Deal three rows of three cards each. These cards are available for building on the foundations.

Play: Start going through the cards in your hand one by one. As soon as an Ace comes up, start a foundation row above the layout. As soon as a 2 comes up, place it in that row also, as shown in the picture.

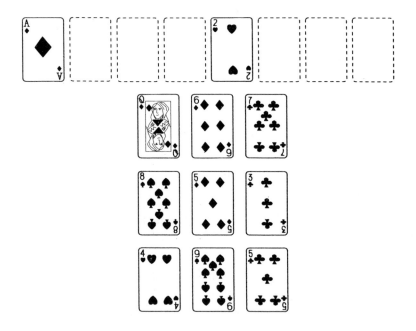

Eventually, you need to place three more Aces and three more deuces in the foundation row. One of each suit should be represented.

If you can't play the card from your hand onto the foundations, put it in a wastepile.

If a space opens up in the group of nine cards, fill it right away from the wastepile, or—if there is none—from your hand.

To win the game: Build the foundations upward in suit to full 13-card sequences—but you need to do it by 2s!

The Aces should build like this:
A 3 5 7 9 J K 2 4 6 8 10 Q

The deuces should build like this:
2 4 6 8 10 Q A 3 5 7 9 J K

Redeals: One.

Panama Canal _____

Other Names: Precedence
Panama
Order of Precedence

Space: Moderate
Level: Easy

This is almost as simple as a game can get.

Layout: The layout starts with only one card in place—a King. That card will be followed by seven additional cards—the Queen, Jack, 10, 9, 8, 7, and 6 of any suit—as they become available. These are foundations.

To win the game: You need to build each foundation downward and regardless of suit into a sequence of 13 cards.

Play: Start going through the pack, one card at a time. The catch is that you have to place the Queen before you can put down the Jack, and the Jack must be in place before you can place the 10, and so on, down to the 6. You are free, though, to build on the cards that are already in place. For example, you can put a Queen on the King that is already on the table and a Jack on the Queen. Unplayable cards go into a wastepile whose top card is always available.

Circular sequence: Kings may be built on Aces when the foundation card is something other than an Ace or King.

Redeals: Two.

Queen of Italy

Other Names: Terrace
                    Signora
Space: Moderate
Level: Easy

Layout: Deal 11 cards at the top, overlapping each other, face up. Then deal three cards face up: you get the opportunity to choose from these three which one will be your foundation. You make this choice based on the 11 cards you've already laid out.

After you decide on a foundation card, put it in place

below and to the left of the first row. Then, use the two cards you did not select for the foundation to start a nine-card row at the bottom. Deal another seven cards from stock. This nine-card row is where the action takes place. You may play

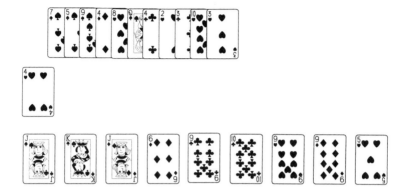

the cards to the foundations as they become available. You can also build them on each other downward in alternating colors. Only one card at a time may be moved from the layout.

To win the game: Build your foundation cards into eight complete 13-card sequences in alternating colors.

Circular sequence: Kings can be built on Aces, if your foundation card is something other than an Ace or King.

What about those 11 cards at the top? They are out of bounds, playable only onto the foundations, as they become exposed.

Play: Start by making what plays you can to the foundations and within the layout. When you can't make any more moves, go through the cards in your hand one at a time. Play what you can to the foundations and the nine-card row. Put unplayable cards in a wastepile. The top card of the wastepile is always available for play.

Spaces in the nine-card row may be filled from the top card of the wastepile or from the stockpile. Never add any cards to the 11-card overlapping row.

Falling Star ————————————————

Play exactly the same as *Queen of Italy*, except:
1. The overlapping row represents stars that have to fall for the game to be won.
2. The next card (the 12th) becomes the foundation.

Blondes and Brunettes ——————————

Other Names: Wood

Play exactly the same as *Queen of Italy*, except:
1. Deal only ten cards in the overlapping row instead of 11.
2. Skip the three-card choice of foundation. The next card becomes the foundation card.
3. Deal nine cards for the bottom row.

General Patience ——————————

Other Names: Thirteen

Play exactly the same as *Queen of Italy*, except:
1. Deal 13 cards instead of 11 for the overlapping row at the top.
2. Build in suit rather than in alternating colors.
3. You do not actually get a redeal, but you are allowed to turn the wastepile over and play until you reach an unusable card. Then the game is over.

Royal Cotillion

Other Names: None
Space: Large
Level: Moderate

There's something especially intriguing about this game, which is not surprising, considering that it is one of the most popular of the two-pack games.

Layout: First, to your left, deal out three rows of four cards each. To your right, deal out four rows of four cards each. Leave a space between them that is wide enough for two cards which will be the foundation columns. As they become available, move one Ace and one deuce of each suit into this center section.

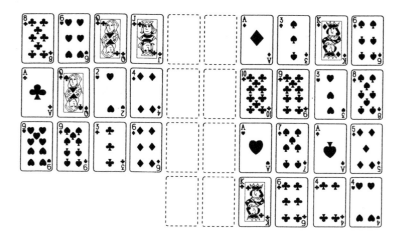

To win the game: Build the Aces and deuces in the middle section upward by suit to a full 13-card sequence. The building must be by twos, as follows.

Aces should build:

A 3 5 7 9 J K 2 4 6 8 10 Q

Deuces should build:

2 4 6 8 10 Q A 3 5 7 9 J K

Play: Go through the cards one by one, building onto the foundations if you can or to the wastepile if you can't.

The cards that are off to your right can all be played onto the foundations, and as soon as spaces open up in this group, you can fill them from the wastepile—or if there is no wastepile, from your hand.

The cards that are off to the left, however, have only one active row—the bottom one. You can't move the cards in the second row until the bottom ones have been moved away. For example, in the illustration, only the 9 of Hearts, the 9 of Spades, the 3 of Clubs, and the 6 of Diamonds would be available to play onto the foundations. Spaces in the left-hand group are never filled in.

Gavotte

Other Names: Odd and Even
Space: Large
Level: Easy

Play exactly the same as *Royal Cotillion*, except:
1. Lay out four rows of four cards on the left as well as on the right.
2. Either the left-hand group or the right-hand group can be the one that moves and is filled in. Take your choice, but whichever way you decide, you need to keep it that way for the whole game.
3. Foundations can be whatever cards you choose—3 and 7, Queen and Jack—whatever.

Royal Rendezvous

Other Names: None
Space: Moderate
Level: Easy

There's enough variety in this game to make it fun, even if there are few surprises!

Layout: First, lay out all eight Aces in two rows, one on top of the other. Each row should have one Ace of each suit. Then lay out one deuce of each suit—two on each side of the bottom row, as in the picture. Underneath this row, deal out two rows of eight cards each. They can be played onto the foundations.

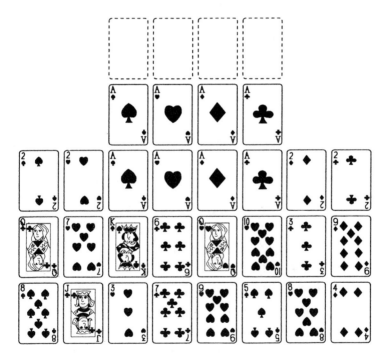

To win the game: Build up all eight Aces and four deuces in suit as follows:

1. The top row of Aces gets built up in suit to Queens.
2. The bottom row of Aces gets built up by twos to Kings, like this:

A 3 5 7 9 J K

3. The deuces get built up by twos to Queens, like this:
2 4 6 8 10 Q

4. Four Kings get put at the top of the layout—but not until after their counterparts have already appeared in the lowest foundation row.

Play: Go through the cards, one by one, and build them onto the foundations if you can. If not, discard them to a wastepile. If a space opens up in the bottom two rows, you must fill it with the top card of the wastepile, or, if there isn't any, with the card from your hand.

St. Helena

Other Names: **Napoleon's Favorite**
Washington's Favorite
Privileged Four
Space: **Moderate**
Level: **Easy/Moderate**

With its odd and changing rules, this game has a peculiar fascination. Maybe that's why Napoleon is said to have played it while in exile. Others say that's unlikely because the game hadn't even been invented then. There's an enormous amount of laying out of cards, but in the end, it's worth it.

Layout: Start by removing one Ace and one King of each suit from the cards and setting them up in 2 rows, Kings on top. These are your foundations.

Then deal out the rest of the pack in 12 piles clockwise: four on top, two on the right side, four on the bottom of the foundations, and two on the left side, as in the illustration.

Keep on dealing, one card on each of the 12 piles, until you've laid out all the cards.

To win the game: Build the Aces up in suit to Kings and the Kings down in suit to Aces.

Play: Only the cards on the tops of the piles can be moved. First, build them onto the foundations; then build them on each other, one card at a time, either up or down, regardless of suit or color. You can reverse direction on the same pile.

When building, only a Queen can go on a King (or vice versa) and only a deuce can go on an Ace.

When you run out of moves, the deal is over.

Special: In the first deal, you are limited in placing cards on the foundations.

1. Only the cards at the sides of the layout can go on any foundation.
2. The cards at the top may be played only to the Kings line.
3. The cards at the bottom may go only on the Aces line. In redeals (you get two of them), any card of the right suit and rank can go on any foundation. You're not limited in this odd way.

Redeals: Two. To redeal, gather the piles counter-clockwise, starting in the upper left-hand corner. Then deal the cards, starting at the left-hand corner, as far as they go.

Louis

Other Names: **St. Louis**
                              Newport
Level: **Moderate**

Play exactly the same as *St. Helena*, except:

1. After you deal the first 12 cards of the piles, play everything you can onto the foundations; then fill the spaces from the stockpile. After that, deal the rest of the cards.
2. All cards in the layout can be played to the foundations without any restrictions—in all deals.
3. Building on the layout piles must be in suit.

Box Kite

Play exactly the same as *St. Helena*, except:
1. There is only one deal, with no restrictions on it.

2. Aces can be built on Kings and Kings on Aces.
3. When the top cards of two foundations of the same suit are in sequence, one or more cards may be transferred onto the other foundation. The original Ace and King may not be transferred, however.

Sly Fox

Other Name: Twenty
Space: Moderate
Level: Easy

Fate or free will? It's free will in this game of choices!

Layout: Set out four Aces—one of each suit—vertically at the left, and four Kings—one of each suit—vertically at the right. Then deal out four rows of five cards between them. The Aces and Kings are foundations on which you are going to build.

To win the game: The Aces need to get built up to Kings, and the Kings down to Aces, by suit.

Play: Build on the foundations using the cards in the middle of the layout. As each space opens up, fill it with a card from your hand.

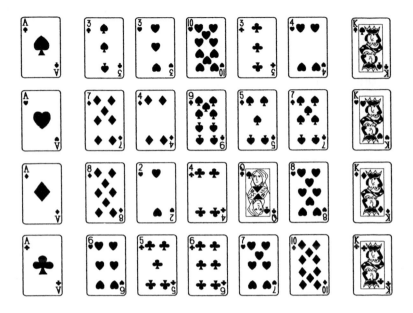

When you can't make any more plays, start going
through the cards, one by one. If you can play a card onto a
foundation, do so. But if you can't, place it on one of the 20
cards that lie between the foundations. You have your choice
of which one. As you place it there, count it (do not count the
ones that you put on the foundations, though).

When you have placed 20 cards on the 20 cards that lie
between the foundations, stop going through the cards.
Now you can make any new plays that have become possible in the layout.

Each time play comes to a standstill, start going
through the cards again. But this time, don't fill the spaces
with cards from your hand. And as before, after you place 20
more "unplayable" cards onto the layout, stop and make the
moves to the foundations that have become possible.

Note: There is no limitation on the number of cards that
you may play to any card in the layout. You could play all 20
on one card, if you wanted to. Or, you can be sly, like a fox!

Colorado

Other Names: None
Space: Large
Level: Easy

Some say this game is *Sly Fox* in sheep's clothing. It is very similar to that game.

Layout: Deal two ten-card rows of cards. Above them, you'll set up a foundation row of four Aces and four Kings, as they become available.

To win the game: Build the Aces up to Kings and the Kings down to Aces in suit.

Play: First, play whatever you can to the foundations. As spaces open up in the layout, fill them at once with cards from the stockpile.

When you've made every move you can, start playing one card at a time from your hand. If the card can't go on the foundation, you can put it on top of any card in the layout.

No card can be moved off the layout except to place on a foundation.

Spider

Other Names: None
Space: Large
Level: Difficult

This game has been called "the king of all solitaires."
Layout: Deal out 54 cards in ten piles as follows: six cards in the first four piles, five in the last six piles. Only the top cards should be face up. These piles are the foundations and the layout at the same time, and all the action takes place on them.

To win the game: Build eight sequences in downward order from Kings to Aces right on the layout. Once a sequence is built, it is discarded. So to win the game is to have nothing on the table.

Play: After you lay out the cards, make all the moves you can, building down, regardless of suit. Note, however, that even though you're *permitted* to build regardless of suit, you limit yourself when you do it. You are permitted to move a group of cards as a unit only when they are in suit and in correct rank—so while you would never be able to win the game by making only moves that were in suit, it is certainly better to build in suit, if you have the choice.

When you move an entire pile, leaving a blank space, you may move any available card or group of cards into it. Keep in mind, though, that a King cannot move, except into a blank space. It cannot be placed on an Ace.

When you can't make any more moves, deal ten more cards, one on each pile. And again, make whatever moves you can. Follow this procedure for the entire game, dealing another ten cards whenever you're stuck.

All spaces must be filled before you are allowed to deal another ten cards onto the layout.

After you have put together a complete sequence, you don't have to discard it right away. You may be able to use it to help build other sequences.

The Sultan of Turkey

Other Names: **The Sultan**
The Harem
Emperor of Germany

Space: Moderate
Level: Easy

Layout: Remove the eight Kings and one Ace of Hearts from the pack and place them as shown in the illustration. Add four cards from the pack on both sides of the Kings. You can use these cards to build onto the foundations.

All the Kings—and the Ace—are foundations, except for the King of Hearts that is in the middle of the square. Don't build on it.

To win the game: Build all the Kings (except the middle King of Hearts) up to Queens, in suit—and build the Ace of Hearts to a Queen, also.

Of course, in order to build up the Kings, you're going to need to add an Ace before starting on the deuces.

Play: Go through the cards one by one and start adding to the foundations. Any cards you can't use go into a wastepile.

As soon as a space opens up in the layout, fill it at once, either from the wastepile or from your hand.

Redeals: Two. Shuffle well before going through the cards a second and third time.

The most delightful aspect of this game is the way it looks when you win. Try it.

Tournament

Other Names: None
Space: Large
Level: Easy/Moderate

Layout: First, deal two columns of four cards each, one to your left, one to your right. These are the "kibitzers." If no Aces or Kings appear among them, put the cards back and deal again.

Next, deal six columns of four overlapping cards each. They are called the "dormitzers."

Then, as they become available, place one Ace and one King of each suit—the foundations—between the kibitzers, as in the illustration.

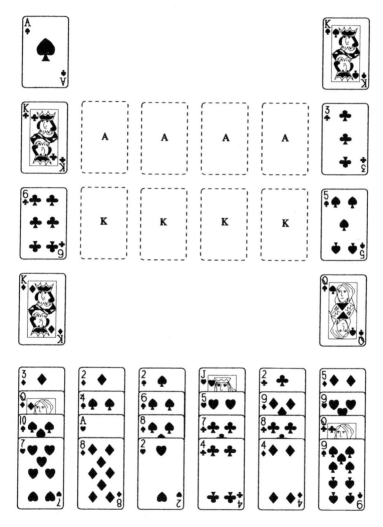

To win the game: Build Aces up to Kings and Kings down to Aces in suit.

All the kibitzers and the exposed cards of the dormitzers are available for playing onto the foundations.

A space in the dormitzers must be filled right away with four cards from the stockpile. A space in the kibitzers may be filled by any available (exposed) card from the dormitzers, but you can do it whenever you want.

Play: Make whatever moves you can from the kibitzers and the dormitzers to the foundations. When there are no more moves to be made, deal another four cards to each of the six piles of the dormitzers. If you have less than 24 cards to deal, that's all right—just put them down as far as they will go.

Reversal: When the top cards of two foundations of the same suit are in sequence, one card may be transferred onto the other.

Redeals: Two. To redeal, pick up just the dormitzers, with the last pile on top.

Weavers

Other Names: Leoni's Own
Space: Moderate
Level: Moderate

Layout: Select from the pack one Ace and one King of each suit. Place them in two rows, Kings on top. These are the foundations.

Now, below them, deal out two rows of six face-up cards each. As you deal them out, count to yourself, "Ace, 2, 3, 4, 5, 6, 7, 8, 9, 10, Jack, Queen, King" (the King space is off to the right, as in the illustration). If the card you name appears as you name it, that card is an Exile. Put it aside at your left, face down. Deal another card in its place, repeating the same card name. In that way, deal out the entire pack of cards.

Exiles

Play: When all the cards are laid out, build what you can to the foundations. All the top cards of the piles are available, plus all the cards in the Kings pile. Spread the Kings pile, so that you can view all the cards at the same time.

Then uncover one card from the cards at your left—the Exiles. If the Exile card can be played onto a foundation, you must play it. If it cannot, place it at the bottom of the pile that corresponds to its number. If it is a 3, for example, slip it under the 3s pile. Then take the top card from the 3s pile—let's say it's a Queen—and slip it under the Queens pile. Continue in this way until you can place something on a foundation. If you turn up a King, however, all play stops.

Slip the King on the bottom of the Kings pile, and turn up the next Exile card.

Reversal: When the Ace foundation and the King foundation of the same suit are in sequence, you are permitted to shift all the cards from one foundation onto the other. Let's say, for instance, that you have built the Ace foundation up to the 6 and the King foundation down to the 7. According to this rule, you could move the 6, 5, 4, 3, and the 2 onto the King foundation. You are not allowed, though, to move the original Ace or King.

Redeals: Two. To redeal, gather the cards up beginning with the Kings pile and go backwards through the cards to the Ace pile, so that Kings are on top, Aces on the bottom.

Windmill

Other Names: Propeller
Space: Moderate
Level: Moderate

There's plenty of action in this hypnotic game, and some strategy is useful.

Layout: Put an Ace in the middle of the design, and then deal two more cards in each direction in the shape of a windmill.

Play: Go through the cards in your hand, one by one. As Kings become available, put them in the angles of the windmill, as shown by the dotted lines. They are the foundations. You will build down on them, regardless of suit. The central Ace is also a foundation. You will build up on it regardless of suit. Put unplayable cards in a wastepile.

To win the game: Build the Kings down to Aces, regardless of suit, and build up the Ace in a continuous sequence (also regardless of suit) until it contains 52 cards—four times through the Ace-to-King sequence.

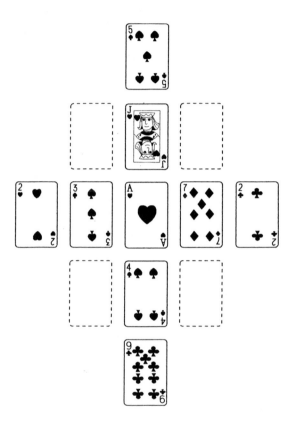

You can use the cards in the windmill shape for foundation building. When a space opens up in the windmill, fill it from the wastepile or, if there is no wastepile, from the cards in your hand.

It is legal to steal the top card from a King foundation to use for the Ace foundation on these conditions: that you use only one card at a time, and that the next card to go on the Ace foundation must come from a regular source.

Informational Chart and Index __

Game	Page	Space			Difficulty			For the very young	# of packs
		S	M	L	E	M	D		
Accordion	14	★	★				★	★	1
Aces Up	16	★				★		★	1
Agnes	48		★			★			1
Alexander the Great	49			★		★			1
All Fours	30		★			★			1
Auld Lang Syne	17	★					★		1
Baker's Dozen	18			★	★				1
Baroness	19		★		★	★		★	1
Beleaguered Castle	20			★	★				1
Betrothal	22			★	★				1
Betsy Ross	23	★				★			1
Big Forty	84			★		★			2
Bisley	24			★		★			1
Blondes and Brunettes	104		★		★				2
Bouquet	40			★	★				1
Box Kite	110		★		★	★			2
British Square	74		★		★				2
Broken Intervals	25	★			★				1
Busy Aces	75	★			★				2
Cadran	84			★		★			2
Calculation	25	★			★				1
Canfield	26	★					★		1
Canfield (wrongly)	46		★				★		1
Capricieuse	76		★		★				2
Captive Queens	63		★		★				1
Chameleon	30	★					★		1
Chessboard	37			★			★		1
Citadel	21			★	★				1
Clock, The	30		★			★			1

INFORMATIONAL CHART AND INDEX

Game	Page	Space			Difficulty			For the very young	# of packs
		S	M	L	E	M	D		
Clover Leaf	49			★		★			1
Colorado	113			★	★				2
Congress	77	★					★		2
Contradance	78	★				★			2
Coquette	22			★	★				1
Corner Card	71	★				★			1
Corners	71	★				★			1
Cotillion	78	★			★				2
Crescent	79			★		★			2
Czarina	71	★				★			1
Demon	26	★					★		1
Demon	46		★				★		1
Demon Triangle	46		★				★		1
Diplomat	81		★		★				2
Double Fan	90			★	★				2
Double or Quits	32	★			★				1
Duchess	33	★				★			1
Duchess of Luynes	88	★				★			2
Eagle Wing	34		★				★		1
Emperor of Germany	115		★		★				2
Fairest	23	★				★			1
Fairest, The	25	★			★				1
Fair Lucy	49			★		★			1
Falling Star	104		★		★				2
Fanny	87		★			★			2
Fan, The	49			★		★			1
Fan, The	82			★	★	★			2
Fascination	26	★					★		1
Fascination	46		★				★		1
Firing Squad	16	★				★		★	1
Fives	37			★			★		1

INFORMATIONAL CHART AND INDEX

Game	Page	Space			Difficulty			For the very young	# of packs
		S	M	L	E	M	D		
Flower Garden	40			★	★				1
Fort	36			★			★		1
Fortress	36			★			★		1
Forty Thieves	82			★		★			2
Four Kings	23	★				★			1
Four of a Kind	30		★			★			1
Four Seasons	71	★				★			1
Fourteen Out	37			★	★				1
Fourteen Puzzle	37			★	★				1
Fourteens	37			★	★				1
Frog	87		★		★	★			2
Gaps	38			★			★		1
Garden, The	40			★	★				1
Gavotte	106			★	★				2
General Patience	104		★		★				2
Glenwood	33	★				★			1
Golf	41		★				★		1
Good Measure	19			★	★				1
Grand Duchess	88	★				★			2
Grandfather's Clock	42			★	★				1
Harem	115		★		★				2
Harp	89			★	★				2
Harvest	44	★					★	★	1
Hidden Cards	30		★			★			1
Hit or Miss	44	★					★	★	1
House in the Wood	90			★	★				2
House on the Hill	91			★	★				2
Hunt	30		★			★			1
Idle Year	14	★	★				★	★	1
Idiot's Delight	16	★				★		★	1
Idiot's Delight	45			★	★				1

INFORMATIONAL CHART AND INDEX

Game	Page	Space			Difficulty			For the very young	# of packs
		S	M	L	E	M	D		
Indian	85			★	★				2
Intelligence	92		★			★	★		2
King Albert	45			★	★				1
King's Audience	64		★		★				1
Klondike	46		★				★		1
Klondike by Threes	47		★				★		1
La Belle Lucie	49			★		★			1
La Francaise	63		★		★				1
Laying Siege	20			★	★				1
Leoni's Own	118		★			★			2
Little Spider	52	★				★			1
Louis	110		★		★	★			2
Lucas	86			★	★				2
Maria	86		★			★			2
Matrimony	22			★	★				1
Matrimony	55		★			★			1
Matrimony	93		★				★		2
Methuselah	14	★	★				★	★	1
Midnight Oil	49			★		★			1
Miss Milligan	85		★				★		2
Monte Carlo	53		★			★			1
Mount Olympus	97		★	★	★				2
Musical	23	★				★			1
Napoleon at St. Helena	84			★		★			2
Napoleon's Favorite	108		★		★	★			2
Napoleon's Square	98		★		★				2
Nestor	55		★			★			1
Newport	110		★			★			2
Number Ten	87			★		★			2
Odd and Even	100		★			★			2
Odd and Even	106			★	★				2

INFORMATIONAL CHART AND INDEX

Game	Page	Space			Difficulty			For the very young	# of packs
		S	M	L	E	M	D		
Open Crescent	80			★		★			2
Order of Precedence	101		★		★				2
Osmosis	56	★				★			1
Panama	101		★		★				2
Panama Canal	101		★		★				2
Parisienne	89	★				★			2
Parterre	40			★	★				1
Partners	63		★		★				1
Patience	17	★					★		1
Peek	57	★				★			1
Perseverance	18			★		★			1
Pile of 28	60		★				★		1
Plus Belle	23	★				★			1
Poker Solitaire	58		★			★			1
Poker Squares	58		★			★			1
Precedence	101		★		★				2
President's Cabinet	77	★					★		2
Privileged Four	108		★		★	★			2
Propeller	120		★			★			2
Pyramid	60		★				★		1
Quadrille	63		★		★				1
Quadruple Alliance	23	★				★			1
Quadruple Line	98		★		★				2
Queen of Italy	102		★		★				2
Queen's Audience	64		★			★			1
Rainbow	29	★					★		1
Rank and File	85			★		★			2
Roll Call	44	★					★	★	1
Roosevelt at San Juan	84		★			★			2
Royal Cotillion	105		★			★			2
Royal Marriage	22			★	★				1

INFORMATIONAL CHART AND INDEX

Game	Page	Space			Difficulty			For the very young	# of packs
		S	M	L	E	M	D		
Royal Rendezvous	107			★		★			2
Russian Solitaire	65			★			★		1
St. Helena	108		★		★	★			2
St. Louis	110		★			★			2
Scorpion	68			★		★			1
Selective Canfield	28	★					★		1
Sham Battle	20			★	★				1
Shamrocks	51			★	★				1
Signora	102		★		★				2
Sly Fox	111		★		★				2
Small Triangle	46		★				★		1
Spaces	38			★			★		1
Spider	114			★			★		2
Spiderette	70		★				★		1
Storehouse	29	★				★			1
Streets	85			★		★			2
Streets and Alleys	21			★	★				1
Sultan	115		★		★				2
Sultan of Turkey	115		★		★				2
Sundial	30		★			★			1
Super Flower Garden	51			★	★				1
Superior Demon	29	★				★			1
Take Fourteen	37			★	★				1
Talkative	44	★					★	★	1
Tam O'Shanter	17	★					★		1
Terrace	102		★		★				2
Thirteen	26	★					★		1
Thirteen	104		★		★				2
Thirteen Down	34		★				★		1
Three Shuffles and a Draw	49			★		★			1

INFORMATIONAL CHART AND INDEX

Game	Page	Space			Difficulty			For the very young	# of packs
		S	M	L	E	M	D		
Thumb and Pouch	49		★		★				1
Toad	87		★		★	★			2
Toad-in-the-Hole	87		★		★	★			2
Tournament	116			★	★	★			2
Tower of Babel	14	★	★				★	★	1
Travellers	30		★			★			1
Treasure Trove	56	★				★			1
Trefoil	51			★	★				1
Treize	44	★					★		1
Triangle	46		★				★		1
Vanishing Cross	71	★				★			1
Washington's Favorite	108		★		★	★			2
Weavers	118		★			★			2
Weddings	53		★			★			1
Whitehead	48		★			★	★		1
Windmill	120		★			★			2
Wings	34		★				★		1
Wood	104		★		★				2
Yukon	67			★		★			1